TREATMENT PLANNER FOR MENTAL HEALTH CHILDREN

Comprehensive Strategies for Nurturing Children's Mental Health, Effective Tools, Interventions, Therapy, Support, Wellness and Development

Brandon Oliver

Brandon Oliver

TABLE OF CONTENTS

INTRODUCTION

When it comes to mental health, kids are like little superheroes, tough yet delicate, figuring out their way through a world that's always changing. From dealing with family stuff to school stress, they face a lot. That's where "Treatment Planner for Mental Health Children" comes in think of it as your trusty guidebook for helping these young minds thrive.

This book isn't just about theory it's packed with real-world strategies that actually work, backed by solid evidence. Whether it's anxiety, depression, trauma, or any other challenge, each part of this book tackles a range of issues. And don't worry, it's not just a bunch of complicated jargon we break it down in a way that makes sense, drawing from the latest research and clinical know-how.

But here's the best part: we're all in this together. The treatment planning process for children's mental health underscores the importance of collaboration. Parents, teachers, therapists each of us has a role to play. With interactive activities and personalized plans, this book gives you the tools to create a nurturing environment where kids can flourish.

So let's roll up our sleeves and get to work, because together, we can help build a brighter future for our little ones.

CHAPTER 1

UNDERSTANDING CHILD MENTAL HEALTH

Encouraging healthy mental development in children fosters positive relationships and facilitates learning and personal growth. However, challenges with mental health can impede a child's progress and affect their overall wellness. Recent data from the Centers for Disease Control and Prevention (CDC) reveals that one in six children aged two to eight grapples with a mental, behavioral, or developmental disorder.

According to licensed child and adolescent social worker Natasha Lee Blair, the prevalence of mental and behavioral health issues has escalated, with a surge in diagnoses observed since the onset of the COVID-19 pandemic. Blair emphasizes the importance for parents to grasp fundamental concepts of childhood mental health, enabling them to recognize early indicators and seek appropriate interventions.

Identifying Mental Health Concerns in Children

While it's normal for children to experience occasional feelings of sadness, anxiety, irritability, or aggression, difficulties in regulating emotions and behaviors could signify underlying issues. Commonly diagnosed mental health conditions among children aged 3 to 17 encompass anxiety disorders, depression, attention-deficit/hyperactivity disorder (ADHD), obsessive-compulsive disorder (OCD), post-traumatic stress disorder (PTSD), autism spectrum disorder (ASD), and eating disorders.

Recognizing signs across age groups

Signs of mental health conditions in young children may manifest differently from those in older age groups. Young children often express negative emotions through anger, but persistent isolation, excessive worrying, or uncontrollable anger are warning signs that necessitate attention. Parents of teenagers should remain vigilant for changes in sleeping and eating habits, as well as indications of self-harm.

Key Indicators in Young Children:

- Frequent irritability or tantrums
- Expressing worries or fears frequently
- Restlessness or inability to stay still
- Social withdrawal or difficulty making friends
- Academic struggles

Signs in Older Children:

- Shifts in mood or behavior, such as withdrawal, anxiety, or irritability
- Loss of interest in previously enjoyed activities
- Social isolation or disengagement from social circles
- Sleep or eating disturbances, excessive exercise, or preoccupation with diet

Ways Parents Can Assist Their Child's Mental Health

Should you observe concerning shifts in your child's behavior persisting for more than a few weeks, seeking additional guidance is advisable. Initiate conversations with individuals regularly interacting with your child, such as teachers or caregivers, to gain insights into their behaviors.

Subsequently, consult your child's healthcare provider regarding their behavior. They can facilitate connections with mental health professionals for accurate diagnosis and recommend suitable interventions, including medication, individual therapy, family counseling, or academic adjustments.

Parental Support Strategies:

1. Foster open communication and establish trust.

2. Educate yourself about your child's mental health condition to comprehend symptoms, treatment alternatives, and effective support methods.

3. Promote healthy lifestyle habits encompassing nutritious eating, regular exercise, and sufficient sleep.

4. Exercise patience, acknowledge your child's strengths, and celebrate their advancements.

For parents grappling with concerns regarding their child's mental well-being, it's crucial to recognize that assigning blame is unwarranted. Mental health challenges can arise from various factors beyond parental control. Seeking assistance and support is encouraged to ensure your child's safety, well-being, and contentment.

CHAPTER 2

IMPORTANCE OF TREATMENT PLANNING FOR MENTAL HEALTH IN CHILDREN

Is the Mental Well-being of Children Important?

Children's mental well-being, a crucial aspect of their overall health, has intricate connections with their physical health and their capacity to thrive in various spheres such as school, work, and society. Both physical and mental well-being influence our internal thoughts and feelings as well as our external behaviors.

For example, a young boy who is overweight and faces teasing about his weight might withdraw socially, leading to feelings of depression. Consequently, he may avoid interacting with others or engaging in physical activity, exacerbating his physical health issues and further impacting his mental well-being. Such challenges can have long-lasting effects on children and adolescents, affecting their potential and influencing various societal systems including health care, education, employment, and the legal system.

Consider a boy named Bobby who experiences physical abuse from his father, resulting in aggressive behavior at school. While his actions stem from his traumatic experiences, they may also indicate an undiagnosed conduct disorder. Unfortunately, Bobby's behavior is misinterpreted by teachers as mere troublemaking, leading to continuous punishment. As a teenager, Bobby drops out of school due to the hostile environment and seeks to escape his abusive home. However, his struggles continue as he faces difficulties in maintaining employment due to his aggression. Bobby turns to alcohol as a form of self-medication, leading to multiple arrests. Only in his thirties does he receive a proper diagnosis, highlighting the missed opportunities for intervention during his childhood.

Every child deserves access to effective care to address and prevent mental health issues. However, there is a significant gap in meeting these needs, particularly for children from low-income backgrounds, ethnic minorities, or those with special needs.

How Prevalent are Mental Health Disorders in Children?

Approximately 15 million young people in the United States can currently be diagnosed with a mental health disorder, with many more at risk due to various factors. Despite the prevalence, only a small percentage of youth in need receive appropriate support from mental health professionals.

The Role of Psychology

Psychological research has contributed to the development of effective treatments and prevention strategies for mental health disorders in children, youth, and families. These interventions operate at multiple levels, including individual, peer, family, school, community, and systemic levels. Psychologists are trained to consider developmental factors, cultural influences, and linguistic diversity when addressing mental health issues in children and adolescents.

Assessment tools developed by psychologists help identify risk and protective factors, monitor treatment progress, and design programs that involve families, schools, and communities. Engaging these social supports is crucial for ensuring lasting well-being for children and youth.

Despite the documented impact of child mental health on development and society, public awareness remains limited. There is a need to recognize the importance of mental health in child development and societal well-being, as well as to promote evidence-based approaches for prevention and treatment.

The Significance of Mental Health in Typical Child Development

Supporting optimal social and emotional development in children yields positive outcomes for both individuals and society, such as improved behavior, enhanced academic performance, stronger relationships, and economic benefits. Stable, responsive caregivers play a crucial role in fostering children's mental well-being, influencing brain development right from birth. It's imperative to provide these caregivers with the necessary support.

Families, caregivers, teachers, and other individuals involved in children's lives should have a better understanding of the normal milestones in healthy child development. This knowledge helps reassure caregivers when development progresses as expected and enables early identification of signs indicating the need for assistance.

Children and families can be equipped to handle stressors and transitions by learning resilience-building skills, thus safeguarding and promoting mental health. Teaching skills and competencies that enhance developmental outcomes to children, parents, and caregivers is essential. Establishing predictable routines at home, in childcare settings, and at school is vital for supporting child mental health.

Efforts must be made to address outcome disparities based on factors such as race/ethnicity, urban versus rural environments, and socioeconomic status. Unfortunately, those most in need or at the highest risk often have limited access to high-quality interventions.

Challenges Faced by Parents in Everyday Life

Interventions aimed at promoting children's mental health can strengthen families and enhance parental skills. Reducing poverty can increase resources available for promoting children's mental health. Integrated one-stop facilities offering comprehensive health care and human services enable parents to address their children's needs, including safety, education, health, and well-being.

The fragmentation of services can hinder parents from fulfilling their children's needs. Enhancing community- and family-based social supports while reducing social isolation and marginalization empowers families, schools, and community agencies to enhance child mental health and foster responsible citizenship.

For families with children diagnosed with mental illness, coordinated systems of care can effectively alleviate the severity of symptoms. Establishing positive and effective communication, active listening, and trusting partnerships between families and schools are essential for promoting children's mental health within the community.

Opportunities for Prevention in Child Mental Health

Prevention strategies targeting multiple risk factors have been shown to reduce the prevalence of mental, emotional, and behavioral disorders in childhood, leading to healthier developmental outcomes. Making healthy prenatal choices, such as avoiding smoking, alcohol, or drug use, and minimizing unintentional toxic exposure, is crucial for protecting the developing brain and promoting child mental health.

Community-wide initiatives employing evidence-based approaches can effectively reduce the incidence of childhood mental, emotional, and behavioral disorders. Consistent prevention messaging across various settings, such as healthcare, childcare, and youth-serving organizations, can yield more impactful results.

Integrating social and emotional learning into school programs not only enhances academic success but also prevents mental health problems. Early intervention to prevent physical and emotional abuse is imperative, and affordable, high-quality childcare should be prioritized and valued.

Effective Treatment Approaches for Childhood Mental Health Challenges

Children may face a diverse range of mental health issues, spanning from persistent conditions to more transient struggles. It's essential that both the diagnosis and treatment of these issues are tailored to consider the child's developmental stage and cultural background. Collaboration between families and healthcare providers is crucial in establishing treatment goals that are measurable and aligned with the child and family's needs and preferences.

While evidence-based practices exist for many childhood mental health conditions, not all conditions have established treatments. Nevertheless, these evidence-based treatments have demonstrated effectiveness in helping children fulfill their potential and easing distress within families. They play a vital role in supporting children's success at home and in school, reducing engagement in problematic behaviors, and fostering positive interpersonal relationships essential for the child's overall well-being.

Despite the presence of evidence-based treatments, children and families often encounter significant barriers when attempting to access them through the healthcare system. These barriers may include a shortage of trained providers, insufficient public funding, limited coverage from private insurance, and the enduring stigma surrounding mental health issues.

Further research is warranted to develop and refine treatment approaches that are effective, developmentally appropriate, and culturally sensitive for childhood mental health concerns. This ongoing research can inform the customization of interventions to address the specific needs of children and families, ultimately closing the disparity between treatment development and its practical delivery to those who require it.

CHAPTER 3
DIVERSITY AND CULTURE IN CHILD MENTAL HEALTH CARE

Families in America hail from various cultural and ethnic backgrounds, shaping their perspectives on the world and approaches to addressing physical or mental health challenges.

Parents often seek guidance and assistance from their social circles, including family, friends, and religious leaders, when their child faces difficulties. When professional mental health intervention is necessary, finding a provider who recognizes the impact of culture on a child's behavior, development, diagnosis, and treatment is crucial. This concept is known as culturally informed or culturally competent care. Other terms used to denote this understanding include 'cultural sensitivity' or 'cultural awareness.'

Culture plays a significant role in how behaviors are interpreted and managed. Cultural competency is vital in addressing various aspects of family life:

- Recognizing behaviors deemed typical or normal within one culture but not necessarily in others.
- Understanding strategies for resolving everyday challenges between children and parents or other family members.
- Acknowledging religious beliefs, practices, and ceremonies.
- Respecting family customs and traditions.
- Addressing conflicts that may arise when children spend more time with friends than with family.
- Appreciating diverse ways of expressing emotions and issues.

Children and families from culturally diverse backgrounds often have unique needs that are not adequately addressed by the current healthcare system. They may encounter difficulties in accessing healthcare providers or face higher rates of medical or mental health conditions. Some children may experience challenges reconciling different values at home and school, especially if their parents were raised in a different cultural milieu. A culturally aware mental health professional endeavors to understand and alleviate these stressors.

Families may prefer to engage with a mental health professional that shares their cultural background or possesses knowledge about their culture. Methods for finding a clinician who aligns with their cultural background include:

- Seeking recommendations within their cultural community.
- Consulting with spiritual or religious leaders, school counselors, or educators.
- Exploring relevant sources such as newspapers, magazines, or websites.
- Contacting local or state mental health agencies.

While a mental health professional may come from a different cultural background, families can facilitate understanding by discussing the following topics:

- Cultural values and religious beliefs.
- Languages spoken at home and school, along with family members' language preferences.
- Traditional healing practices or remedies.
- Parenting styles and disciplinary methods.

- The significance of family and community in a child's life.
- Cultural expectations regarding children's behavior at different stages.
- Norms regarding the expression of emotions within the family and community.
- The family's experiences with immigration or transitioning to a new culture.
- Addressing losses and traumas associated with immigration or transitioning.
- Factors hindering access to mental healthcare, including transportation, financial constraints, and cultural beliefs.
- Managing conflicts between the child and older generations of the family.
- Recognizing and harnessing the cultural strengths of the child and family.

Below are some actions that your mental health provider can take to ensure culturally competent care:

- Collaborating with your cultural, community, or religious organizations with your consent.

- Assisting parents and caregivers in utilizing behavioral management techniques aligned with their beliefs and values.

- Involving non-blood relatives in assessment and treatment upon the family's or child's request.

- Recognizing effective therapy approaches and medications for youths from specific diverse groups.

- Acknowledging and addressing cultural biases that may impede treatment.

- If your mental health provider doesn't speak your preferred language, arranging for an interpreter or translator, as using friends or family members, including your

child, is not recommended for
interpretation.

Regardless of the language spoken, a culturally
sensitive mental health professional can better
grasp your family's perspective and provide
guidance that respects your values and beliefs.
Sharing details about your family's cultural
background and values will enable the
clinician to tailor a plan to assist your child
effectively.

Brandon Oliver

CHAPTER 4

COMMON MENTAL HEALTH DISORDERS IN CHILDREN

Attention Deficit Hyperactivity Disorder (ADHD)

ADHD stands out as one of the prevalent neurodevelopmental disorders in children, often persisting into adulthood. Children and adolescents grappling with ADHD encounter challenges in maintaining focus, sustaining attention on tasks, and regulating their energy levels and behavior. Some may additionally exhibit hyperactivity, struggling with patience and remaining still.

Other manifestations encompass being easily diverted, issues with organization and task completion, inattentiveness, careless errors, frequent forgetfulness, susceptibility to boredom and frustration, along with excessive talking and interruption. Diagnosis of ADHD hinges on these symptoms surpassing the norm for the individual's age and developmental stage, with behaviors being markedly pronounced and persistent.

Anxiety Disorders

Anxiety disorders encompass a spectrum of mental health conditions that can induce fear, distress, excessive worry, and unease in children. While experiencing anxiety is a typical part of childhood, persistent and severe anxieties can impede daily functioning.

Children and adolescents with anxiety disorders may also exhibit irritability, restlessness, and physical symptoms like headaches or stomachaches. Panic attacks, characterized by symptoms such as shortness of breath and rapid heart rate, are not uncommon. Various types of anxiety disorders exist, including Generalized Anxiety

Disorder and Obsessive Compulsive Disorder (OCD).

Generalized Anxiety Disorder entails persistent worry about everyday matters, often accompanied by perfectionism and seeking reassurance. Children with this disorder may withdraw from social activities and struggle with initiating new tasks due to fear of failure. OCD involves intrusive thoughts (obsessions) leading to repetitive behaviors (compulsions) aimed at alleviating anxiety. These rituals can consume significant time and hinder normal activities, often leading to social withdrawal and difficulty communicating emotions.

Panic Disorder

Panic disorder is identified when a child undergoes at least two unanticipated panic or anxiety attacks, followed by a month of apprehension about experiencing another attack. These attacks arise suddenly without any discernible trigger.

Phobic Disorders

Phobic disorders arise when a child harbors an exaggerated and overwhelming fear of a specific object or situation.

Specific Phobias

Specific phobias entail an intense, irrational fear of a particular object or circumstance, such as animals, storms, medical procedures, heights, or darkness. Affected children typically seek to avoid feared stimuli, experiencing overwhelming anxiety when confronted with them.

Posttraumatic Stress Disorder (PTSD)

PTSD manifests following exposure to a traumatic or life-threatening event. Children with PTSD may exhibit intense fear, anxiety, emotional numbing, irritability, and avoidance behaviors, accompanied by flashbacks, nightmares, and changes in mood and behavior.

Separation Anxiety Disorder

Separation anxiety involves excessive distress when separated from home or caregivers, often leading to extreme homesickness and avoidance of school, camps, or sleepovers. Affected children fear harm befalling their caregivers when apart.

Social Anxiety Disorder

Social anxiety disorder manifests as an intense fear of social or performance situations, hindering social interactions and academic success. Children with social phobia dread being judged or embarrassed in social settings, impeding their participation in everyday activities.

Selective Autism

Selective autism is characterized by an inability to speak in specific social situations, despite being capable of communication in familiar settings. Affected children may exhibit physical signs of anxiety and withdrawal when faced with the expectation to speak.

Bipolar Disorder

Bipolar disorder, or manic-depressive illness, disrupts mood, energy, and activity levels in young individuals, causing extreme fluctuations. Periods of intense lows, known as depression, alternate with episodes of heightened energy and euphoria, termed mania. Symptoms of mania include decreased need for sleep, excessive talking, and impaired judgment. Additional signs may include irritability, racing thoughts, risky behavior, and hallucinations. Treatment and support are vital for managing symptoms and enabling success in various aspects of life.

Conduct Disorder

Conduct disorder is classified among disruptive behavior disorders, characterized by aggression, deceitfulness, and disregard for others' feelings. Individual with conduct disorder may engage in bullying, theft, or property destruction, often exhibiting defiance towards authority figures and struggling with academic and social functioning.

Depression

Depression in children and youth manifests as persistent sadness, loss of interest in activities, and feelings of hopelessness. Other symptoms include fatigue, difficulty concentrating, and withdrawal from social interactions. Physical complaints like headaches or stomachaches may also accompany depressive episodes. Early intervention and treatment are crucial for addressing this serious but manageable condition.

Oppositional Defiant Disorder (ODD)

ODD, another disruptive behavior disorder, involves recurrent episodes of anger and defiance towards authority figures. Individuals with ODD may exhibit unwarranted hostility, blame others for their actions, and resist complying with rules or requests. These behaviors can impede social relationships and academic progress, necessitating intervention to foster positive growth and development.

Eating Disorders

Eating disorders disrupt a child's or adolescent's eating habits significantly, resulting in extreme consumption patterns. Those with eating disorders may display diminished self-esteem, mood swings, and obsessive preoccupation with weight and food. Anorexia nervosa involves an obsession with weight control through starvation or excessive exercise, while bulimia nervosa involves secretive binge-eating followed by purging behaviors. Recovery necessitates essential treatment and support.

Psychosis

Psychosis signifies a severe brain ailment characterized by a detachment from reality. Individuals in a psychotic state may struggle to differentiate between what is real and hallucinations or delusions. Psychosis can manifest in various mental health conditions, including bipolar disorder and schizophrenia, as well as during substance intoxication.

Schizophrenia

Schizophrenia is a grave psychiatric condition marked by disordered thinking, emotions, and behaviors. Symptoms may encompass mood swings, peculiar behaviors, hallucinations, and severe anxiety. Treatment options exist to manage symptoms and foster stability.

Substance Abuse

Substance abuse disorder arises when a young individual repeatedly uses substances that impair daily functioning and create ongoing legal and interpersonal difficulties. Substance use may serve as a means to self-medicate untreated mental health issues.

Tourette's Syndrome

Tourette's syndrome is a neurological disorder resulting in involuntary sounds and movements, referred to as tics. Motor tics include actions like eye blinking or head jerking, while vocal tics may present as throat clearing or shouting. In rare instances, tics may involve inappropriate vocalizations.

Reactive Attachment Disorder

Reactive attachment disorder is an infrequent yet severe condition characterized by unhealthy attachment patterns with caregivers. Children with this disorder may display destructive behavior, absence of guilt or remorse, and manipulative tendencies. Treatment aims to nurture healthy relationships and enhance behavior.

Importance of early intervention

A misconception exists that mental health problems are exclusive to adults, yet children are also susceptible. Mental health disorders can manifest in children as young as three years old, with anxiety disorders, ADHD, and mood disorders being commonly diagnosed. Early recognition of these conditions is crucial to minimizing their potential negative impact on a child's life.

Essential Early Intervention

Early intervention entails promptly identifying and offering services, therapies, and support to children with mental health disorders and their families. This proactive approach yields several advantages:

Enhancing Long-Term Outcomes

Timely intervention significantly improves a child's life trajectory and overall well-being. Given children's ongoing growth and brain development, interventions can effectively prevent the exacerbation of issues and future complications.

Equipping with Skills and Strategies

Early intervention not only addresses immediate concerns but also equips children with lifelong coping strategies. Vital skills like stress management, emotional regulation, and effective communication are imparted.

Supporting Families

This approach also provides invaluable support to families, empowering parents and caregivers with the necessary tools and knowledge to understand and assist their child effectively.

The Role of Schools and Parents in Early Intervention

Schools play a critical role as children spend a substantial portion of their day in educational settings. Educators and counselors can be trained to identify potential signs of mental health issues. Parents, as primary observers, play a significant role in detecting changes in their child's behavior, mood, or social interactions. If concerns arise, seeking guidance and support from professionals.

CHAPTER 5

THE SIGNIFICANCE OF PSYCHOLOGICAL EVALUATION FOR CHILDREN

Psychological assessment holds significant importance in grasping and aiding the mental and emotional welfare of children. Through the utilization of psychological assessment instruments, experts can gather valuable insights into a child's cognitive capabilities, emotional health, and behavioral tendencies. This section will delve into why psychological assessment is crucial and the advantages it provides for children.

Importance of Psychological Assessment

Psychological assessment is indispensable as it offers a thorough evaluation of a child's psychological well-being. It facilitates the identification of strengths, weaknesses, and areas necessitating intervention. Through a comprehensive assessment, psychologists can gain profound insights into a child's unique requirements and tailor interventions accordingly.

Moreover, psychological assessment aids in diagnosing various mental health conditions such as ADHD, ASD, and learning disabilities. Early detection of these conditions enables timely intervention and support, thereby enhancing outcomes for children.

Benefits of Psychological Assessment for Children

Psychological assessment offers numerous benefits for children, parents, and professionals involved in their care. Some key advantages include:

1. Accurate diagnosis and treatment planning: Psychological assessment enables professionals to precisely diagnose mental health conditions and develop personalized treatment plans. This ensures that interventions are targeted and efficacious, addressing the specific needs of each child.

2. Identification of strengths and weaknesses: Psychological assessment helps pinpoint a child's strengths, enabling professionals to capitalize on these positive attributes. It also highlights areas where a child may struggle, guiding interventions to bolster their growth in these domains.

3. Insights into cognitive abilities: Assessing a child's cognitive abilities furnishes valuable information about their intellectual potential. This aids in educational planning, identification of giftedness, or detection of learning disabilities that may require additional assistance.

4. Monitoring progress and treatment outcomes: Psychological assessment tools empower professionals to monitor a child's progress over time. By consistently evaluating their functioning, clinicians can assess the effectiveness of interventions and make necessary adjustments to optimize outcomes.

5. Enhanced communication and collaboration: The assessment process fosters collaboration among professionals, parents, and educators. By sharing assessment findings, all parties involved in a child's care can collaborate to devise effective strategies and support systems.

By acknowledging the importance of psychological assessment and employing appropriate assessment tools, professionals can offer comprehensive care and support for children's mental and emotional well-being. Psychological assessment serves as a valuable tool that unlocks each child's potential, guiding interventions and nurturing their overall development and success.

Factors to Consider When Selecting Assessment Tools

Choosing psychological assessment tools for children requires careful consideration of several key factors to ensure the accuracy and validity of the assessment. Various elements such as suitability for different age groups, the trustworthiness and accuracy of information, consideration of cultural nuances, and the convenience and accessibility of the resource are taken into account.

1. Age Appropriateness: Selecting assessment tools that are suitable for the child's age group is crucial. Children of different ages have varying cognitive and developmental abilities, so it's essential to choose tools that align with their developmental stage. Age-appropriate tools consider factors such as language skills, attention span, and cognitive abilities to provide reliable results.

2. Validity and Reliability: The validity and reliability of assessment tools are fundamental considerations. Validity assesses how well the tool measures what it claims to measure, while reliability evaluates the consistency and stability of results over time. It's important to choose tools with strong evidence supporting their validity and reliability through rigorous research and validation studies.

3. Cultural Sensitivity: Cultural sensitivity is vital when selecting assessment tools for children from diverse cultural backgrounds. Each culture possesses distinct norms and beliefs which play a significant role in shaping the development and conduct of a child. It's essential to choose tools that have been validated and normed using diverse populations to ensure their applicability across different cultural contexts.

4. Practicality and Ease of Use: Assessment tools should be practical to administer and score efficiently. Consider factors such as the time required for administration, the expertise needed to interpret results, and the availability of support materials. Choose tools that fit well within your professional setting and workflow and are user-friendly to enhance the assessment process's efficiency and accuracy.

Collaborating with Professionals

Child psychology assessment tools should be handled by experts in the field for accurate interpretation. Collaboration with psychologists, coaches, and practitioners enhances insights.

Consulting with Psychologists

Psychologists specialize in assessing and understanding human behavior, including children. They possess extensive knowledge of psychological assessment tools and can recommend suitable ones for specific purposes. Psychologists can administer and interpret assessments, providing a comprehensive understanding of a child's functioning.

Working with Coaches and Practitioners

Coaches and practitioners in child development and education can contribute valuable insights to the assessment process. They often have specialized expertise in areas such as educational coaching or behavioral interventions and can provide information about the child's functioning in real-world contexts. Collaborating with psychologists, coaches, and practitioners ensures a holistic approach to psychological assessment for children.

When selecting professionals to collaborate with, ensure they are qualified and experienced in the specific area of assessment required. Their expertise will contribute to the accuracy and usefulness of assessment results, leading to more effective interventions and support for children.

CHAPTER 6

THERAPEUTIC APPROACHES AND INTERVENTION STRATEGIES FOR ADOLESCENTS' MENTAL WELL-BEING

Developing effective treatment strategies for mental health concerns in pre-teens and teenagers begins with a comprehensive mental health evaluation. This initial assessment is crucial for identifying the specific challenges impacting your child's mental well-being.

Subsequently, a tailored treatment plan is devised to enhance your child's overall well-being and alleviate their symptoms. This plan aims to capitalize on your child's strengths while addressing areas of difficulty or triggers exacerbating their symptoms.

As part of the treatment regimen, mental health professionals may recommend specific therapeutic modalities. It's important for parents to actively engage in discussions with the professional, asking pertinent questions and taking notes during appointments. Additionally, seeking further clarification via phone calls is encouraged.

Outlined below are several common therapeutic interventions:

Acceptance and Commitment Therapy (ACT): Derived from cognitive-behavioral therapy, ACT incorporates mindfulness techniques alongside other strategies. Through ACT, adolescents learn to accept elements beyond their control and recognize the impact of these realities on their thoughts and emotions. Moreover, they're guided to acknowledge the appropriateness of their emotional responses to various situations.

Central to ACT is the exploration of personal values, empowering adolescents to align their behaviors with these values.

Behavior Therapy: An integral component of cognitive-behavioral therapy, behavior therapy focuses on modifying an adolescent's behaviors. Therapists devise tailored activities to help adolescents cultivate coping skills for challenging scenarios. Employing a systematic approach, therapists assist adolescents in navigating difficult emotions and situations step by step.

Cognitive-Behavioral Therapy (CBT): CBT is a structured therapeutic approach that acknowledges the interplay between thoughts, emotions, and behaviors. It empowers adolescents to recognize and challenge unproductive thinking patterns and behavior habits. By consciously altering their thoughts, adolescents can positively influence their emotions and behaviors. CBT is effective in addressing various issues such as anxiety, depression, anger management, substance abuse, and eating disorders. It can be administered individually, in group settings, or online.

Counseling: Counseling, often referred to as "talk therapy," provides adolescents with a platform to discuss their concerns in a supportive environment. Rather than offering direct advice, counselors facilitate adolescents in exploring their situations, making informed decisions, and devising solutions. Typically conducted on a one-on-one basis, counseling empowers adolescents to navigate their challenges autonomously.

Creative Therapies: Creative psychotherapies, including art, music, and dance/movement therapy, offer alternative avenues for adolescents to cope with emotional, relational, or behavioral issues. These therapies enable adolescents to express themselves and communicate their experiences in novel and constructive ways, particularly beneficial for those who struggle with verbal expression.

E-Therapies: E-therapies, also known as online or computer-aided psychological therapies, leverage digital platforms to deliver interventions such as CBT and behavior therapy. These programs equip adolescents with tools to identify and modify maladaptive thinking and behavioral patterns contributing to anxiety and stress. While e-therapies can be effective for adolescents with mild to moderate concerns, they may not be suitable for those experiencing acute crises or severe distress.

Family Therapy: In family therapy, practitioners engage both the adolescent and significant family members to facilitate healing and foster relational support. Recognizing the significance of familial bonds in the recovery process, therapists encourage family members to consider each other's perspectives, experiences, and beliefs. Collaboratively, families explore constructive approaches to supporting one another and resolving challenges.

Interpersonal Therapy: Interpersonal therapy (IPT) is a form of psychotherapy rooted in the understanding that interpersonal dynamics can significantly impact mental well-being. The primary objective of IPT is to assist adolescents in comprehending how their social interactions and relational challenges, such as those encountered at school or in personal relationships, influence their mental health. Through IPT, therapists support adolescents in enhancing their communication abilities and regulating their emotions.

Medication: Certain mental health conditions in pre-teens and teenagers may be managed with medication, which can help alleviate symptoms. When a medical professional prescribes medication for your child, it is typically integrated with other therapeutic interventions and support systems to facilitate recovery. It's important to inquire about potential side effects associated with mental health medications, enabling both you and your child to make informed decisions regarding their usage. In most cases, if a mental health professional prescribes medication for a child with a mental health condition, the child usually has the autonomy to decide whether to take it.

Mindfulness: The benefits of mindfulness practices have been well-documented in adults, with studies indicating that techniques like mindfulness-based stress reduction (MBSR) can mitigate stress and improve overall mental well-being. Similarly, mindfulness-based cognitive therapy (MBCT) has shown efficacy in preventing depression recurrence and can be as effective as antidepressant medication. There is a growing body of evidence suggesting that mindfulness interventions are also beneficial for children and teenagers.

Psychotherapy: Psychotherapy aims to enhance your child's understanding of their challenges. Both cognitive-behavioral therapy (CBT) and counseling fall under the umbrella of psychotherapy. In psychotherapy sessions, a trained therapist engages in dialogue with your child, delving into their thoughts and emotions. Together, the child and therapist work on reframing thought patterns and exploring interpersonal dynamics to develop adaptive coping strategies. While psychotherapy is commonly conducted on a one-on-one basis, it can also occur in group settings or involve family members.

Monitoring and Follow-Up: Throughout your child's mental health therapy journey, periodic reviews with the general practitioner (GP) may be necessary, especially if your child is following a formal Mental Health Treatment Plan. Collaborating with other mental health professionals involved in your child's care, the GP monitors progress to ensure the effectiveness of the therapy. Should concerns arise regarding your child's mental health progress, you are encouraged to communicate these with your child's mental health professional or GP. Depending on your child's response to treatment, alternative approaches may be suggested, or the current treatment plan may be continued. Upon completion of therapy, reflecting on your child's progress and acknowledging their achievements can be beneficial.

CHAPTER 7

CLINICAL INTERVIEWS AND OBSERVATIONS

Child Anxiety Overview: Understanding, Evaluation, and Treatment

Defining Child Anxiety

Child anxiety denotes an excessive and persistent apprehension or fear that surpasses typical concerns experienced during childhood development. It transcends regular worries, leading to intense and uncontrollable emotions that disrupt daily functioning and overall well-being.

Forms of Child Anxiety

Child anxiety manifests diversely, encompassing generalized anxiety disorder (GAD), separation anxiety disorder, social anxiety disorder, specific phobias, and panic disorder, each presenting distinctive characteristics and symptoms.

Impact on Development

Child anxiety profoundly influences various facets of a child's development, including emotional stability, social interactions, academic performance, and overall life satisfaction. It impedes socialization, hindering relationship formation and maintenance, while also impeding academic engagement, affecting focus, concentration, and performance.

Assessment and Understanding

Recognizing the ramifications of child anxiety is pivotal for effective intervention and support. Early identification enables tailored assistance, fostering resilience and growth. Parents, caregivers, and professionals play vital roles in discerning signs and symptoms, ensuring appropriate measures are taken to address the challenges faced by anxious children.

Signs and Symptoms

Child anxiety manifests through an array of physical, behavioral, and emotional cues, encompassing symptoms like stomachaches, headaches, muscle tension, fatigue, sleep disturbances, increased heart rate, sweating, dizziness, and nausea. Prompt recognition and consultation with healthcare professionals are essential for accurate evaluation and intervention.

Behavioral Symptoms

Child anxiety profoundly influences behavior and daily activities. Common behavioral manifestations of child anxiety encompass avoidance behaviors, excessive worrying, restlessness, irritability, clinginess, tearfulness, school refusal, perfectionism, difficulty concentrating, and nervous habits.

Emotional Symptoms

Child anxiety exerts a notable impact on emotional health. Emotional manifestations frequently linked with child anxiety encompass excessive fear or worry, restlessness, feeling overwhelmed, irrational fears, low self-esteem, emotional deregulation, panic attacks, mood swings, social withdrawal, and difficulty with transitions.

Seeking Professional Guidance

If your child exhibits these emotional symptoms, seeking guidance from a qualified healthcare provider is imperative. Professional assessment can determine symptom severity and provide tailored support and intervention strategies.

Recognizing the signs and symptoms of child anxiety empowers parents, caregivers, and healthcare professionals to offer timely support and intervention. Early identification and intervention are crucial for enhancing a child's well-being and equipping them with effective coping mechanisms to manage anxiety.

The Significance of Assessment

Understanding child anxiety necessitates a thorough assessment to grasp the challenges faced by affected children comprehensively. By conducting a comprehensive evaluation, healthcare professionals can gain insights into the child's experiences, symptoms, and unique requirements. This section elucidates the importance of assessing child anxiety and elucidates various assessment methods employed.

Importance of Assessing Child Anxiety

Assessment of child anxiety serves several critical purposes. Firstly, it aids in gauging the severity and impact of anxiety symptoms on the child's daily functioning. This evaluation helps professionals understand the extent of functional impairment experienced by the child, encompassing difficulties in academic performance, social interactions, and daily activities. By assessing anxiety's impact, healthcare professionals can devise tailored strategies to assist the child in managing their anxiety and enhancing overall well-being.

Secondly, assessment establishes a baseline measure for tracking treatment progress. Regular assessments enable healthcare professionals to monitor changes in symptoms, functioning, and treatment outcomes over time. This ongoing evaluation facilitates adjustments to treatment approaches as necessary, ensuring that the child receives personalized and effective care.

Types of Assessments for Child Anxiety

Various assessment methods are employed to evaluate child anxiety, involving data collection from multiple sources, including the child, parents, teachers, and healthcare professionals. Below are common assessment techniques:

1. Questionnaires and Surveys: These standardized tools comprise a series of questions aimed at measuring anxiety symptoms and related factors. Responses from the child, parents, or teachers offer valuable insights into the intensity of the child's anxiety symptoms and their impact on daily life.

2. Clinical Interviews: Facilitated by healthcare professionals, clinical interviews entail face-to-face discussions with the child and their parents. This interaction delves deeper into the child's anxiety symptoms, triggers, and overall impact, providing contextual information crucial for assessment and treatment planning.

3. Observation and Behavioral Assessments: These assessments involve observing the child's behavior across various settings, such as school or home. By identifying anxiety-related behaviors like avoidance, excessive worry, or physical symptoms, professionals gain a comprehensive understanding of the child's anxiety and its impact on daily functioning.

By employing a combination of these assessment methods, healthcare professionals obtain a holistic understanding of the child's anxiety symptoms and needs. This comprehensive evaluation serves as the foundation for designing effective treatment and support strategies tailored to the individual child's requirements.

Common Assessment Tools

Assessing child anxiety is vital for addressing the challenges children face effectively. Several assessment tools are available to gather comprehensive information about a child's anxiety levels and related symptoms. Here, we'll explore three common assessment tools: questionnaires and surveys, clinical interviews, and observation and behavioral assessments.

Questionnaires and Surveys

These tools consist of questions designed to gather information about a child's anxiety symptoms, thoughts, and behaviors. Caregivers, parents, and teachers often complete these assessments, providing valuable insights into the child's anxiety across different settings. Questionnaires and surveys allow for standardized assessment, aiding in determining symptom severity and guiding treatment planning.

Clinical Interviews

Conducted by trained healthcare professionals, clinical interviews involve in-depth conversations with the child and their caregiver. This interactive process allows for a comprehensive evaluation of the child's anxiety symptoms, triggers, and impact on daily functioning. Clinical interviews provide personalized insights essential for tailoring treatment plans to meet the child's specific needs.

Observation and Behavioral Assessments

These assessments entail direct observation of the child's behavior in various settings to understand their anxiety-related behaviors. Professionals observe the child's actions, reactions, and responses to different situations, identifying specific triggers and coping mechanisms. Observation and behavioral assessments provide real-time data, offering valuable insights into the child's anxiety and contributing to effective treatment planning.

Challenges in Assessing Child Anxiety

Assessing child anxiety poses several challenges that necessitate careful consideration and evaluation to ensure accurate identification and effective intervention. This section delves into three key challenges: validity and reliability of assessment tools, cultural considerations, and differentiation from other conditions.

Validity and Reliability

The cornerstone of assessing child anxiety lies in utilizing assessment tools that demonstrate both validity and reliability. Validity ensures that an assessment accurately measures what it intends to measure, while reliability ensures consistency and stability of results over time. These qualities are indispensable for obtaining precise information about a child's anxiety levels.

Various assessment tools are available, including questionnaires, surveys, clinical interviews, and behavioral assessments, each serving a unique purpose in gathering information about a child's symptoms and experiences. Selecting validated and reliable tools specifically designed for assessing child anxiety is paramount.

Questionnaires and surveys, such as the Child Anxiety Scale or Child Anxiety Questionnaire, offer a structured approach to gauge anxiety symptoms in children. Clinical interviews, facilitated by trained professionals, allow for a more comprehensive exploration of a child's anxiety experiences. Observation and behavioral assessments provide valuable insights into how anxiety manifests in a child's behavior.

By ensuring the validity and reliability of assessment tools, healthcare professionals can obtain accurate information about a child's anxiety, guiding the development of tailored treatment strategies.

Cultural Considerations

Assessing child anxiety must also consider cultural factors that may influence how anxiety manifests and is perceived within different communities. Cultural norms, values, and beliefs can shape a child's expression of anxiety symptoms and their willingness to disclose them.

Healthcare professionals must be culturally sensitive and aware of potential cultural biases when assessing child anxiety. This involves considering cultural differences in symptom presentation, understanding culturally specific stressors, and adapting assessment approaches accordingly.

Differentiation from Other Conditions

Another challenge in assessing child anxiety lies in differentiating it from other conditions that may present with similar symptoms. Conditions such as attention-deficit/hyperactivity disorder (ADHD), autism spectrum disorder (ASD), or mood disorders can overlap with anxiety symptoms, complicating diagnosis and treatment.

To accurately differentiate child anxiety from other conditions, healthcare professionals must conduct thorough assessments, considering the child's developmental history, symptom duration and severity, and the presence of comorbid conditions. Collaboration with multidisciplinary teams and utilization of comprehensive assessment approaches are essential in addressing these challenges.

Cultural Considerations

When assessing child anxiety, cultural factors significantly influence how anxiety is perceived and expressed. Considering cultural differences is essential to ensure assessments are culturally sensitive and capture the nuances of a child's experience. Certain cultures may prioritize somatic symptoms over emotional ones, while differences in communication styles and help-seeking behaviors can also impact assessment outcomes. To conduct culturally sensitive assessments, it's vital to be aware of biases, understand cultural norms, and adapt assessment techniques accordingly. This approach fosters trust and accuracy in assessments.

Effective Treatment Approaches

Addressing child anxiety requires effective treatment approaches tailored to each child's needs. Therapy options such as Cognitive-Behavioral Therapy (CBT), exposure therapy, play therapy, and family therapy have shown positive outcomes in helping children cope with anxiety. A multidisciplinary approach involving psychiatrists, psychologists, pediatricians, and school counselors ensures comprehensive care. Creating a supportive environment at home and school, characterized by active listening, established routines, self-care practices, and healthy coping mechanisms, enhances the effectiveness of treatment strategies. By combining assessment with appropriate treatment approaches and fostering a supportive environment, children can effectively manage their anxiety and thrive despite its challenges.

CHAPTER 8

AUTISM SPECTRUM DISORDERS

Autism Spectrum Disorder (ASD) is a condition impacting social skills, communication, and behavior, typically emerging within the first few years of life. Symptoms vary in severity and can be attributed to a blend of genetic and environmental factors.

Individuals with ASD commonly exhibit two main categories of symptoms:

1. Challenges in social communication and interaction.

2. Repetitive and restricted behavioral patterns.

These symptoms persist across different settings and cannot be attributed solely to the individual's age-related developmental stage. For instance, while some children may naturally become more reserved during puberty, the manifestations of ASD go beyond typical developmental changes, causing significant disruptions in daily functioning.

Social-communication difficulties associated with ASD encompass:

• Delayed or unusual language development, including scripted speech patterns derived from external sources like television or movies.

• Impaired conversational skills, such as disregarding conversational norms like taking turns speaking or showing limited interest in others' perspectives.

• Difficulty sharing interests, thoughts, and emotions, coupled with a lack of social awareness regarding appropriate behavior.

• Unusual facial expressions, avoidance of eye contact, and peculiar body language.

• Limited use of gestures during interactions and challenges in interpreting others' non-verbal cues.

• Struggles in forming and maintaining close relationships, often due to a lack of interest in social engagement or difficulty adjusting behavior to align with social norms.

Repetitive and restricted behaviors associated with ASD include:

• Engaging in repetitive movements or fixating on specific objects.

• Echoing words or phrases repetitively.

• Resistance to changes in routine or environment, coupled with rigid thinking patterns.

• Developing intense and atypical interests.

• Heightened or reduced sensitivity to sensory stimuli, such as pain, temperature, texture, smell, taste, light, or sound.

Children with autism or other neurodevelopmental disorders may exhibit self-injurious behavior (SIB), characterized by self-directed actions leading to physical harm. While non-suicidal in nature, SIB presents significant challenges in understanding and managing. Resources and support are available for parents navigating their child's experiences with SIB, offering insight into effective strategies and coping mechanisms.

ASD and Mental Health

Challenges and stressors are common for families with children diagnosed with ASD, impacting both the child and the family. However, effective treatment can significantly alleviate these difficulties.

Diagnosing mental illness in children with ASD poses challenges due to overlapping symptoms and the unique presentation of mental health issues within this population. Symptoms of one disorder may mimic those of another, making it challenging to distinguish between them. Additionally, the internal experiences of children with ASD might be difficult to discern, as they may struggle to articulate their emotions. Moreover, external observers might misinterpret the child's behaviors, and the child themselves may not perceive anything amiss. Diagnostic tools specific to mental illnesses in children with ASD are limited, further complicating the process.

Notably, many studies on mental health and ASD primarily involve children with high-functioning autism, who face fewer cognitive or intellectual challenges. Consequently, there's a scarcity of research focusing on the mental health of children classified as lower functioning" or more severely affected by ASD symptoms. It's crucial to recognize that certain groups of children might be excluded from these studies.

Recognizing signs of mental illness in children with ASD can be perplexing, as symptoms overlap with those of ASD itself and other mental health conditions. Consulting a healthcare professional is advisable if there are concerns regarding changes in the child's behavior or emotional state, particularly if such changes persist despite ongoing ASD treatment. Medical evaluations may be necessary to rule out underlying medical issues contributing to behavioral changes.

Various mental illnesses are prevalent among individuals with ASD, with anxiety disorders being particularly common. Anxiety symptoms often manifest differently in individuals with ASD, potentially exacerbating social challenges and communication difficulties. Understanding the co-occurrence of anxiety and ASD requires further research into potential biological and environmental factors.

Anxiety disorders commonly observed in children with ASD include obsessive-compulsive disorder (OCD), generalized anxiety disorder (GAD), social anxiety disorder, specific phobia, and separation anxiety disorder. OCD, characterized by intrusive thoughts and compulsive behaviors, may share similarities with repetitive behaviors seen in ASD. Similarly, GAD can significantly impact a child's daily life, affecting concentration and overall well-being. Phobias, particularly common in children with ASD, may include fears related to sensory sensitivities or social interactions. Separation anxiety disorder can disrupt everyday activities and cause distress when apart from caregivers.

Attention-deficit/hyperactivity disorder (ADHD) is another prevalent condition among children with ASD, with symptoms overlapping with those of ASD, such as difficulties with attention and hyperactivity. Depression, characterized by persistent feelings of sadness and hopelessness, is also common among individuals with ASD, often exacerbated by social challenges and anxiety. Schizophrenia, although less common, can present with hallucinations, delusions, disorganized thoughts, and emotional difficulties in children with ASD.

Overall, understanding and addressing the complex interplay between ASD and mental health disorders require comprehensive assessment and tailored interventions to support the well-being of affected individuals and their families.

CHAPTER 9

PLAY THERAPY TECHNIQUES

Play therapy serves as a crucial therapeutic approach primarily designed for children. This is because children often struggle to process their emotions independently or communicate their issues effectively to parents or other adults.

Although it might seem like simple playtime, play therapy offers a deeper level of engagement.

Skilled therapists utilize playtime as an opportunity to observe and comprehend a child's underlying issues. From there, they can assist the child in exploring emotions and addressing unresolved trauma. Through playful activities, children acquire new coping mechanisms and learn to manage inappropriate behaviors.

Play therapy is administered by various licensed mental health professionals, including psychologists, psychiatrists, behavioral and occupational therapists, physical therapists, and social workers.

Furthermore, the Association for Play Therapy provides specialized training programs and advanced certifications for licensed mental health professionals, school counselors, and school psychologists.

Benefits of Play Therapy

According to Play Therapy International, as many as 71 percent of children undergoing play therapy exhibit positive changes.

Although some children may initially exhibit hesitancy, their trust in the therapist typically grows over time. As rapport strengthens, children often become more expressive and creative during play sessions.

Some potential advantages of play therapy include:

• Assuming accountability for specific behaviors

• Developing coping strategies and innovative problem-solving skills

• Cultivating self-respect and empathy towards others

• Mitigating anxiety and fostering emotional expression

• Enhancing social and familial relationships

Additionally, play therapy can promote language development and improve both fine and gross motor skills.

It's important to note that if your child has a diagnosed mental or physical condition, play therapy should complement rather than replace any prescribed medications or essential treatments. It can be utilized independently or alongside other therapeutic modalities.

When to Use Play Therapy

While individuals of all ages can benefit from play therapy, it's typically applied to children between the ages of 3 and 12. Play therapy proves beneficial in various circumstances, including:

- Coping with medical procedures, chronic illness, or palliative care
- Addressing developmental delays or learning disabilities
- Managing problematic behaviors at school
- Dealing with aggression or anger issues

- Navigating family challenges such as divorce, separation, or bereavement
- Tackling mental health concerns like anxiety, depression, or grief
- Addressing eating or toileting disorders, ADHD, or ASD.

How Play Therapy Functions

There exists a notable communication barrier between children and adults. Due to differences in age and developmental stages, children often lack the linguistic abilities of adults. Consequently, they may experience emotions they struggle to articulate to adults or lack a trusted individual to confide in.

Conversely, adults may misinterpret or overlook both verbal and nonverbal cues from children.

Play serves as the primary means through which children comprehend the world and their role within it. During play, they freely express their innermost feelings and emotions. Toys, acting as symbols, carry significant meaning, provided one knows how to interpret them.

Given the child's limited ability to express themselves in the adult realm, therapists bridge this gap by engaging with the child on their own terms and within their realm of play.

As children engage in play, they often become less guarded and more inclined to share their emotions. Importantly, they are not coerced but given the space and time to communicate in their own manner.

Approaches to play therapy vary depending on the therapist and the child's specific needs. Initially, therapists may observe the child at play and conduct individual interviews with the child, parents, or educators.

Following a comprehensive assessment, therapists establish therapeutic objectives, delineate necessary boundaries, and devise a plan for intervention.

Therapists closely monitor how children manage separation from their parents, their solo play, and their response upon reunification with their parents.

Significant insights can be gleaned from observing a child's interactions with various toys and tracking changes in behavior across sessions. Children may utilize play to confront fears, alleviate anxieties, or engage in healing and problem-solving.

Therapists leverage these observations to inform subsequent interventions, tailoring therapy to meet each child's unique requirements. As therapy progresses, behaviors and objectives are subject to reassessment.

At certain junctures, therapists may involve parents, siblings, or other family members in play therapy, a practice known as filial therapy. This approach facilitates conflict resolution, fosters healing, and enhances familial dynamics.

Techniques in Play Therapy
Sessions typically span 30 minutes to an hour and occur weekly or at similar intervals. The duration of therapy depends on the child's responsiveness and engagement with the therapeutic process.

Play therapy can be either directive or nondirective. In the directive approach, therapists guide the session by selecting toys or games and directing play toward specific goals.

Conversely, the nondirective approach is less structured, allowing children to choose toys and engage in play autonomously with minimal intervention. Therapists observe closely and intervene as appropriate.

Sessions occur in environments where children feel secure and encounter minimal constraints. Therapists may employ techniques such as creative visualization, storytelling, role-playing, toy-based activities, artistic expression, sensory play with water and sand, construction activities, dance, and musical engagement.

Examples of Play Therapy
Play therapy encompasses a wide array of methods tailored to each child's needs and circumstances. Therapists may guide children towards specific play techniques or allow them to choose freely, depending on the

situation. Below are some examples of how play therapy can be employed:

1. Dollhouse Therapy: The therapist provides a dollhouse and dolls, inviting the child to act out familial or interpersonal conflicts they may be experiencing at home.

2. Puppet Play: Children can use hand puppets to recreate stressful or frightening situations, providing a safe space to explore and express their emotions.

3. Storytelling: Children may be encouraged to tell stories or read books that reflect their experiences, a technique known as bibliotherapy. This can help them articulate their feelings and find solutions to their problems.

4. Artistic Expression: Therapists may engage children in drawing or painting activities while asking probing questions to gain insights into their thoughts and emotions.

5. Game Play: Various games can be used to promote problem-solving, cooperation, and social skills development in children.

Play Therapy for Adults

Play therapy isn't limited to children; it can also benefit teenagers and adults who struggle to express their emotions verbally. Here are some scenarios where play therapy for adults can be beneficial:

1. Dramatic Role-Playing: Adults may engage in role-playing exercises to explore and address difficult emotions or past traumas in a safe environment.

2. Sand-Tray Therapy: This technique involves using miniature figurines and a tray of sand to create scenes that represent inner thoughts, feelings, and experiences.

3. Art Therapy, Music Therapy, and Movement: Activities like drawing, music, and dance can help adults relax, uncover hidden traumas, and promote healing.

4. Complementary Therapy: Play therapy can be used alongside other forms of therapy and medication to address various mental health issues.

5. Tailored Approach: Just like with children, play therapy for adults is tailored to individual needs and circumstances, ensuring personalized care and support.

Finally, play therapy is a versatile method that uses play to address psychological issues in both children and adults. It can be used as a standalone therapy or in conjunction with other interventions. To benefit fully from play therapy, it's essential to seek out a licensed mental health professional experienced in this approach. Referrals can be obtained from pediatricians, primary care doctors, or through resources like the Association for Play Therapy.

CHAPTER 10

IMPORTANCE OF EMOTIONAL REGULATION IN CHILDREN

Emotional regulation pertains to a child's capacity to manage their emotions, thoughts, and actions. Sophie Havighurst and Ann Harley devised the Tuning in to Kids initiative, which advocates for emotionally attuned parenting. They assert that emotional regulation is a vital component of a skill set necessary for handling one's own emotions and responding to those of others, often referred to as emotional competencies or emotional intelligence. These skills encompass:

1. Understanding one's own emotions and effectively communicating them to others.

2. Recognizing and interacting with the emotions of others, particularly in emotionally charged situations.

3. Regulating one's own emotions, including controlling, expressing, and adjusting them appropriately to cultural and situational contexts.

4. Utilizing emotions to achieve personal objectives.

Why is emotional regulation important?
Emotional regulation holds significant importance in children's daily lives as it influences their comprehension of situations, their responses, behavior, and overall enjoyment of life. Assisting children in comprehending and managing their emotions equips them with skills they will utilize in adulthood. Emotional intelligence is crucial because:

1. It fosters awareness and control over one's actions.

2. It reduces stress levels, correlating with improved health outcomes.

3. It facilitates more fulfilling friendships and enduring intimate relationships.

4. It enables self-soothing, allowing individuals to calmly focus, concentrate, and think amid challenging circumstances, thereby enhancing resilience and easing the handling of change and stress.

Parenting Counts additionally suggests that children who grasp their emotions and learn about them:

- Forge stronger friendships.
- Quell their distress more swiftly.
- Perform better academically.
- Manage their moods adeptly, experiencing fewer negative emotions.

- Experience fewer instances of illness.

Is emotional regulation innate or taught?
Acquiring the necessary skills for emotional regulation constitutes a significant developmental task for children. They rely on adult support to achieve this, much like newborns need assistance in regulating basic needs such as body temperature, heart rate, and sleep. Learning emotional regulation skills is a gradual process that commences at birth and extends into adulthood.

The development of emotional skills varies among children. Kids Matter suggests that younger children may exhibit a higher level of emotional development compared to older children, who might take longer to acquire the skills necessary to manage their emotions. Additionally, cultural factors can influence how children regulate their emotions.

In infancy, recognizable emotions include joy, anger, sadness, and fear. As children begin to form a sense of self, more complex emotions like shyness, surprise, elation, embarrassment, shame, guilt, pride, and empathy emerge. Primary school-aged children are still in the process of learning to identify emotions, understand their origins, and appropriately manage them. Initially, young children's emotions primarily manifest as physical reactions (e.g., increased heart rate, butterflies in the stomach) and behaviors. With growth and development, children gain the ability to recognize feelings more explicitly.

Self-regulation, distinct from intelligence, is influenced by various factors:

Age: Self-regulation matures as children age.

Biology: A child's temperament and responses to stress affect the development of self-regulation.

Relationships: Interactions with caregivers, including how they accommodate the child's temperament and respond to their needs, shape self-regulation.

Cognition: Language use, especially in naming emotions, aids in self-regulation development and lays the foundation for future learning.

Parents and caregivers serve as crucial role models for children's emotional regulation development. Observing adults effectively regulate their emotions helps children learn to manage their own feelings and behaviors. Over time, children gradually learn to regulate their emotions independently.

Children often express emotions through behavior due to their developmental stage or lack of verbal expression. The Circle of Security parenting program emphasizes understanding the emotional needs behind children's behavior.

Additional issues such as trauma can impact children's emotional regulation and their families. Trauma, resulting from threatening, violent, or life-challenging events, can hinder emotional understanding, expression, and social cue recognition.

How are emotional regulation and school readiness linked?

Self-regulation skills identified by Blair et al. promote learning and school adjustment. These skills include focusing attention, regulating emotions and stress responses, reflecting on information and experiences, and engaging in positive social interactions.

Emotional regulation facilitates:

Intentional focus despite distractions, problems, or excitement.

Laying the groundwork for academic achievement and social-emotional competence, essential for a successful school transition.

How can parents assist their children in developing skills for emotional regulation?

Parents can aid their children in mastering emotional regulation by:

• Providing structure and predictability.

• Modeling self-control and regulation, especially when experiencing frustration, upset, or excitement.

• seeking assistance if a child struggles with emotional or behavioral management, ensuring early identification and intervention.

What parents can do

• Act as exemplars in handling emotions.

• Reflect on how they handle their own emotions.

• Demonstrate understanding and validation of their child's emotions, showing empathy towards them.

• Take their child's emotions seriously and strive to understand their perspective.

Developing crisis intervention plans
• A Mental Health Crisis arises when immediate action or intervention is necessary, or when the child is deemed unsafe to themselves or others.

• Crisis situations can be highly stressful, frightening, and exhausting for both the child/youth and the involved family.

• Crisis planning serves as a proactive approach to help restore balance for the child and family.

• A crisis plan is tailored to the individual and crafted from the strengths, preferences, and natural resources of the child and family.

Why Develop a Crisis Plan?

• Children and youth should receive support in the least restrictive clinically appropriate environment.

• It helps identify positive strategies to prevent escalation and determine the subsequent steps if behaviors do escalate.

• Provides early intervention and support.

• Facilitates identification of support and guidance from various sources such as family members, friends, therapists, or mental health providers.

• It's a plan owned by the child and family, reflecting their definition of a crisis within their family.

• It's a dynamic document that can be revised and utilized proactively to prevent future crisis situations.

• What to Consider When Developing a Crisis Plan

• Optimal timing for developing a crisis plan is when the child and family are in a calm and stabilized state.

• Define how the child and family perceive a crisis.

• Identify past situations that escalated into a crisis and the interventions that effectively de-escalated those situations.

• Determine individuals and resources whom the child and family feel supported by, and consider preferences for informal, formal, or self-managed support.

• Ensure the plan also prioritizes the safety of other family members in the household.

Managing a Mental Health Crisis

• During a crisis, individuals, including children, may struggle to articulate their thoughts, feelings, and emotions, or comprehend communication from others. Assess the situation as a parent or caregiver to determine if emergency assistance, guidance, or support is needed, and whether the child is at immediate risk of harming themselves, others, or property.

• For some children, the fight or flight response may dominate during a crisis, leading to sudden, reckless, and potentially dangerous actions. This can leave families and caregivers feeling frightened and bewildered.

• If it becomes necessary to transport the child, consider if it can be done safely. If not, explore whether a support person is available to assist. If transportation is deemed unsafe and no assistance is available, inform the destination about the situation and inquire about recommended actions.

- If you believe your child or family is facing immediate danger, dial 911 and request law enforcement assistance.

- Inform law enforcement that assistance is needed for a child or youth experiencing a mental health crisis or emergency, increasing the likelihood that an officer trained in handling mental health issues will respond.

- When providing details about the situation, be specific about observed behaviors and current circumstances.

- Expect the police officer to inquire about the youth's diagnosis, medications, hospitalization history, and any legal background.

- Note that once 911 is contacted and a police officer arrives, they assume control of the situation, including decisions regarding your child's placement.

• As the caregiver, you can advocate for the officers to approach the situation from a mental health crisis perspective and provide input on desired outcomes.

Reflect - What Just Happened?

• Following a crisis, it's crucial to debrief with the youth, family, caregivers, and treatment team to identify potential triggers or causes of the crisis and assess the effectiveness of interventions used.

• Recommendations for preventing and managing future crises can be integrated into the crisis plan.

• The team will address and treat underlying conditions contributing to the crisis behaviors.

• This is an opportune time to review medications and any adjustments made during Emergency Department or hospital visits, if applicable.

• Family members should document concerns to discuss with the treatment team during the debriefing.

• Advocating for a person with mental illness during a crisis can be challenging due to healthcare privacy laws and provider interpretations. Family members may need the individual's consent to communicate with the treatment team effectively.

CONCLUSION

In wrapping up this extensive guide to treatment planning for children's mental health, it's crucial to highlight the importance of personalized interventions and collaborative approaches in meeting the various needs of this guide. Throughout this text, we've delved into a range of evidence-based strategies, methods, and interventions aimed at nurturing the mental well-being of children and adolescents.

A central takeaway go beyond the significance of embracing a holistic perspective that acknowledges the intricate interplay of developmental, social, and environmental factors shaping a child's mental health. By grasping the interconnectedness of these elements, mental health professionals can craft tailored treatment plans that delve into the underlying causes of distress while fostering resilience.

Moreover, the vital role of teamwork among multidisciplinary professionals cannot be overstated. Effective treatment planning often hinges on the collective input of psychologists, psychiatrists, social workers, educators, and other specialists collaborating to support a child's overall welfare. Through synergy of expertise and resources, these teams can offer comprehensive care that addresses the multifaceted needs of young clients.

This book also underscores the critical importance of cultural competence and sensitivity in mental health practice. Appreciating and honoring the cultural backgrounds, beliefs, and values of children and their families is paramount for cultivating trust and nurturing effective therapeutic bonds.

As we draw this journey through treatment planning for children's mental health to a close, let's remain steadfast in our commitment to evolving our practices in tandem with emerging research, shifting societal landscapes, and evolving clinical insights. By maintaining a steadfast dedication to the well-being of children and adolescents, we can pave the way for meaningful progress in promoting mental health and fortitude in future generations.